SINGLED OUT WORKBOOK EXPERIENCE

A PATH TO CLARITY AND PURPOSE

TIANA T. BURNETT

EDITED BY
NICOLE QUEEN

VISION PUBLISHING HOUSE

*To every single person who has ever questioned her strength,
her worth, or her purpose, this companion workbook is for you.*

*May these pages be a consecrated space for
reflection, healing, and rediscovery.*

CONTENTS

INTRODUCTION

Welcome to the *Singled Out Workbook Experience: A Path to Clarity and Purpose* — the official companion to the book *Singled Out: A Journey of Faith, Resilience, and Strategic Guidance*. This companion workbook was prayerfully created to walk hand in hand with you as you read the book, reflect on your journey, and take bold, faith-filled steps toward healing and purpose.

Whether you're a single mom, a married woman, a woman of faith, or someone navigating your own "singled out" season, this experience is designed to meet you where you are.

Each chapter provides guided teaching moments, journal reflections, scripture reflections, action steps, and space to write your truth. You'll also find group activities to support deeper connection in women's ministries, small groups, or coaching settings.

This is a launching pad for clarity, transformation, and unapologetic purpose. Let's begin the journey — one chapter, one reflection, one purpose-driven step at a time.

CHAPTER 1
THE CONCEPT OF SINGLED OUT
RECOGNIZING GOD'S HAND IN SEPARATION

This chapter invites you to take a second look at the moments you've been "singled out"—not as setbacks, but as signs that God's hand is gently, intentionally guiding you toward purpose. Reframe your understanding of separation as purposeful!

* * *

TEACHING MOMENT

Being singled out by God doesn't always feel comfortable—it can feel lonely, confusing, and even painful. But separation is often God's preparation. Throughout scripture, we see how isolation became the launching pad for transformation. Moses, Joseph, Esther, and David— each had moments of being "set apart" for something greater.

We often view isolation as punishment or consequence—but in God's hands, separation is sanctification. It's a divine invitation to go deeper, grow stronger, and be positioned for something greater. The Bible is full of stories where people were set apart before they were sent forth: Moses in the wilderness, Joseph in prison, Esther in the palace, David in the fields. God uses the quiet seasons to shape character, clarify identity, and prepare us for impact. You haven't been cast aside — you've been called apart. *Could it be that God is using your season of solitude to align you with your purpose?*

JOURNAL REFLECTION

Reflect on the questions below. Use the lines provided to write honestly and prayerfully.

1. When have you felt "singled out" in life?

_____

_____

_____

_____

_____

_____

_____

_____

2. How did those experiences shape your faith or direction?

_____

_____

_____

_____

_____

_____

_____

_____

3. Can you identify divine patterns in your personal story?

_____

_____

_____

_____

_____

_____

_____

_____

SCRIPTURE MEDITATION

 Before I formed you in the womb, I knew you, before you were born I set you apart...

— JEREMIAH 1:5

Take a moment to pause, reflect, and handwrite the scripture on the lines below.

_____

_____

_____

_____

_____

_____

What does this verse mean to you personally?

_____

_____

_____

_____

_____

_____

_____

_____

_____

_____

_____

_____

_____

_____

_____

_____

_____

ACTION STEPS

List 3 times you felt isolated:

1. _____
2. _____
3. _____

Identify what good came from those moments:

_____
_____
_____
_____
_____

List 2 people in scripture who were also "singled out":

1. _____
2. _____

Write a prayer thanking God for setting you apart:

_____
_____
_____
_____
_____
_____
_____
_____

REFLECTION SUMMARY

How does being singled out feel different when you see it as divine design?

_____

_____

_____

_____

_____

_____

_____

_____

_____

_____

_____

_____

_____

_____

_____

_____

_____

_____

_____

_____

_____

_____

_____

_____

_____

_____

_____

_____

_____

GROUP ACTIVITY: *"CIRCLE OF STRENGTH"*

1. Have each woman write down a moment when she felt "singled out" but experienced God's presence.
2. Go around the circle and share these moments aloud.
3. After each share, have the group affirm each speaker by declaring together: *"You were never alone."*
4. End with a unified prayer of thanksgiving, inviting God to continue revealing purpose through every moment of separation.

Use the space below to jot down any key reflections from this group experience.

_____
_____
_____
_____
_____
_____
_____
_____
_____
_____
_____
_____
_____
_____
_____
_____
_____
_____
_____
_____
_____

CHAPTER 2
THE SINGLED OUT JOURNEY
TRUSTING THE PROCESS OF BECOMING

This chapter is your reminder that becoming takes time. Growth happens in layers. Even when it feels like nothing is changing, God is still working behind the scenes, preparing you for what's ahead. You are not stuck—you are becoming. And every season is shaping your strength, sharpening your vision, and stretching your faith.

* * *

TEACHING MOMENT

The journey of becoming all God created you to be isn't linear—it unfolds in divine rhythm. Sometimes we're called to wait. Other times we're healing. Some seasons are about building, and others are when we begin walking in what we've prepared for. But in each season, God is present, refining us for greater purpose.

In scripture, we see how God used each phase of a person's life to mold them. Joseph's betrayal led to promotion. Ruth's grief led to redemption. David's tending of sheep led to the throne. The hidden places are not wasted—they're holy. Embrace the process. Trust that your steps, even the slow or painful ones, are aligned with a greater destiny.

JOURNAL REFLECTION

Reflect on the questions below. Use the lines provided to write honestly and prayerfully.

1. What season are you currently in — waiting, healing, building, or walking? Why?

_____

_____

_____

_____

_____

_____

_____

_____

2. Have you seen progress in your life, even if it's slow? Describe it.

_____

_____

_____

_____

_____

_____

_____

_____

_____

3. What part of your journey are you still questioning?

_____

_____

_____

_____

_____

_____

_____

_____

SCRIPTURE MEDITATION

 To everything there is a season, and a time to every purpose under the heaven...

— ECCLESIASTES 3:1

Take a moment to pause, reflect, and handwrite the scripture on the lines below.

_____

_____

_____

_____

_____

_____

What season do you feel God is guiding you through right now?

_____

_____

_____

_____

_____

_____

_____

_____

_____

_____

_____

_____

_____

_____

_____

_____

_____

ACTION STEPS

Identify your current season:

- ☐ Waiting
- ☐ Healing
- ☐ Building
- ☐ Walking

Write one lesson that you've learned from your current season:

_____

_____

_____

_____

_____

_____

_____

_____

Reflect on someone else's journey who inspired you: Who are they, and what did you learn from them?

_____

_____

_____

_____

_____

_____

_____

_____

List three promises God has made to you (personal or from scripture):

1. _____

2. _____

3. _____

REFLECTION SUMMARY

How is your journey uniquely preparing you for your next assignment?

_____
_____
_____
_____
_____
_____
_____
_____
_____
_____
_____
_____
_____
_____
_____
_____
_____
_____
_____
_____
_____
_____
_____
_____
_____
_____
_____
_____
_____

GROUP ACTIVITY: *"SEASONS OF BECOMING"*

Create four labeled stations in your space: *Waiting, Healing, Building,* and *Walking.* Provide sticky notes and pens. Each participant should walk through each station and add a note pertaining to:

- An experience they've had in that season
- A lesson they've learned
- A word of encouragement for others

Debrief: After everyone has rotated through, gather and discuss:

- Which season was hardest?
- Which season revealed the most growth?
- What are you learning about your current place in the process?

Close in prayer, thanking God for the beauty in every season of becoming.

Use the space below to jot down any key reflections from this group experience.

_____
_____
_____
_____
_____
_____
_____
_____
_____
_____
_____
_____
_____
_____
_____
_____

CHAPTER 3
NAVIGATING CHALLENGES
FROM STUCK TO STRATEGY

This chapter is your invitation to shift— to lean into faith instead of fear. To make small, intentional steps that lead to big transformation. God isn't asking for perfection—just your participation. With every prayer, every decision, every act of courage, you're moving forward. You're not stuck—you're being positioned for strategy.

* * *

TEACHING MOMENT

One of the enemy's greatest tactics is to convince us that being stuck is our final destination. But the truth is, God often does His best work when we feel most uncertain. The key is shifting your mindset from fear to faith. Instead of asking "Why me?" begin asking, "What is God trying to show me through this?"

Scripture reminds us that God's grace is sufficient—even in weakness. That means our limitations are not liabilities, they're launching pads for divine strength. When you replace limiting beliefs with biblical truths and take one small step at a time, you begin to gain momentum. And with God as your strategist, no obstacle is too great to overcome.

JOURNAL REFLECTION

Reflect on the questions below. Use the lines provided to write honestly and prayerfully.

1. What's your biggest current challenge right now?

_____

_____

_____

_____

_____

_____

_____

_____

2. What do you say to yourself in hard times? Are your thoughts helpful or harmful?

_____

_____

_____

_____

_____

_____

_____

_____

_____

3. How have past challenges shaped your strength, faith, or mindset?

_____

_____

_____

_____

_____

_____

_____

_____

_____

SCRIPTURE MEDITATION

 My grace is sufficient for you, for My strength is made perfect in weakness...

— 2 CORINTHIANS 12:9

Take a moment to pause, reflect, and handwrite the scripture on the lines below.

_____
_____
_____
_____
_____
_____

How does this verse speak to your current situation?

_____
_____
_____
_____
_____
_____
_____
_____
_____
_____
_____
_____
_____
_____
_____
_____
_____
_____

ACTION STEPS

List 3 limiting beliefs you currently hold:

1. _____
2. _____
3. _____

Now, replace each one with a scripture-based truth:

1. _____
2. _____
3. _____

Set a simple goal for this week (small + doable):

1. _____
2. _____
3. _____

Identify 3 support resources (people, places, or tools):

1. _____
2. _____
3. _____

Commit to one action per day (or every three days) this week that moves you toward your goal:
(Check off each day you took action and write out what you did.)

☐ Monday: _____
☐ Tuesday: _____
☐ Wednesday: _____
☐ Thursday: _____
☐ Friday: _____
☐ Saturday: _____
☐ Sunday: _____

REFLECTION SUMMARY

What do you now understand about navigating life's challenges through faith, not fear?

_____

_____

_____

_____

_____

_____

_____

_____

_____

_____

_____

_____

_____

_____

_____

_____

_____

_____

_____

_____

_____

_____

_____

_____

_____

_____

_____

_____

_____

_____

GROUP ACTIVITY: *"FAITH STRATEGY CIRCLE"*

1. Break into small groups of 3–5.
2. Have each woman share one current challenge she's facing.
3. Have the group help brainstorm: one mindset shift rooted in scripture or faith and one practical action step they can take this week.
4. Come back together as a large group and share one key insight or "aha moment" from each small group. Encourage one another, speak life, and pray together.

Use the space below to jot down any key reflections from this group experience.

_____
_____
_____
_____
_____
_____
_____
_____
_____
_____
_____
_____
_____
_____
_____
_____
_____
_____
_____
_____
_____
_____
_____

CHAPTER 4
LIVING OUT YOUR PURPOSE
WALKING BOLDLY IN WHAT YOU'RE CALLED TO DO

This chapter is a reminder: you don't have to have it all figured out to begin. Purpose isn't about perfection—it's about obedience. God often uses the parts of our stories that we tried to hide—the pain, the doubts, the detours—as the very soil where purpose takes root. When you say yes to the assignment, you're saying yes to transformation. You're saying yes to becoming.

* * *

TEACHING MOMENT

Walking in purpose requires boldness, not because we're fearless, but because we trust the One who called us. Throughout scripture, we see ordinary people with flawed pasts doing extraordinary things because they obeyed. Moses stuttered. Esther feared the risk. David was underestimated. But God used them anyway—and He's ready to use you too.

Your purpose isn't defined by your resume, but by your willingness to say yes. It's less about your qualifications and more about your surrender. When you choose obedience over hesitation, God multiplies your impact. He takes your "yes" and turns it into influence, healing, breakthrough—for yourself and for others.

JOURNAL REFLECTION

Reflect on the questions below. Use the lines provided to write honestly and prayerfully.

1. What is your "why"—the reason behind what you do and how you serve others?

_____

_____

_____

_____

_____

_____

_____

2. Have you ever felt unqualified or unprepared for what God asked of you? How did you respond?

_____

_____

_____

_____

_____

_____

_____

_____

3. Think back to a moment when you felt fully alive and in alignment with your purpose. What were you doing? Who were you helping?

_____

_____

_____

_____

_____

_____

SCRIPTURE MEDITATION

> Many are the plans in a person's heart, but it is the Lord's purpose that prevails.

— PROVERBS 19:21

Take a moment to pause, reflect, and handwrite the scripture on the lines below.

_____

_____

_____

_____

_____

_____

What does this verse teach you about trusting God's bigger plan?

_____

_____

_____

_____

_____

_____

_____

_____

_____

_____

_____

_____

_____

_____

_____

_____

_____

ACTION STEPS

Identify 3 talents or passions God has placed within you. If you're unsure, ask someone who knows you well to share what gifts they see in you:

1. _____
2. _____
3. _____

Reflect on how you've used each in the past: (Example: "I've encouraged women through writing...")

_____
_____
_____
_____

Write the definition of "purpose" in your own words:

_____
_____
_____
_____

Craft a short purpose statement for your current season: (Example: "I believe I'm called to...")

_____
_____
_____
_____

Choose and complete at least one purposeful act this week:

☐ Volunteering
☐ Writing or speaking to uplift someone
☐ Encouraging someone
☐ Starting a passion project
☐ Other: _____

REFLECTION SUMMARY

How is your obedience opening doors for your purpose to unfold?

_____
_____
_____
_____
_____
_____
_____
_____
_____
_____
_____
_____
_____
_____
_____
_____
_____
_____
_____
_____
_____
_____
_____
_____
_____
_____
_____
_____
_____

GROUP ACTIVITY: *"PURPOSE DECLARATION"*

1. Provide each participant with a decorative worksheet that prompts them to complete the sentence: *"I am called to..."*
2. Allow 10–15 minutes of quiet reflection and writing.
3. Invite volunteers to stand and read their purpose statements aloud to the group.
4. After each declaration, have the group clap, affirm, or repeat: *"Walk in it, Queen!"* or *"Purpose unlocked!"*
5. Close with a group prayer, asking God to ignite boldness, clarity, and obedience in every woman as she walks out her purpose.

Use the space below to jot down any key reflections from this group experience.

_____

_____

_____

_____

_____

_____

_____

_____

_____

_____

_____

_____

_____

_____

_____

_____

_____

_____

_____

CHAPTER 5
ADDRESSING COMMON CRITICISMS
SILENCING THE VOICES OF DOUBT

This chapter is about reclaiming your mind and guarding your heart. It's about replacing lies with truth, and learning to recognize the difference between conviction from God and condemnation from others. What people said about you may have left scars, but what God says about you holds power. You are chosen. You are equipped. You are enough.

* * *

TEACHING MOMENT

Most of us have faced criticism—sometimes constructive, but often destructive. And if left unchecked, those words can become internalized beliefs that limit our growth. The enemy would love for you to live your life based on someone else's broken opinion of you. But God invites you to renew your mind with His truth.

Scripture tells us that no weapon formed against us shall prosper (Isaiah 54:17). That includes word curses, harsh labels, and limiting beliefs. You were not created to live bound by others' expectations. You were created to walk in freedom and truth. When you silence the noise and elevate God's voice, you rediscover the bold, powerful, anointed version of yourself that was there all along.

JOURNAL REFLECTION

Reflect on the questions below. Use the lines provided to write honestly and prayerfully.

1. What have others said about you that wounded you? How did it affect your confidence or decisions?

_____
_____
_____
_____
_____
_____
_____

2. What does God say about you in contrast to those criticisms?

_____
_____
_____
_____
_____
_____
_____
_____

3. How do you typically respond to criticism — with silence, defensiveness, hurt, or strength?

_____
_____
_____
_____
_____
_____
_____

SCRIPTURE MEDITATION

 No weapon formed against you shall prosper...

— ISAIAH 54:17

Take a moment to pause, reflect, and handwrite the scripture on the lines below.

_____

_____

_____

_____

_____

How does this scripture reshape how you receive and respond to words spoken against you?

_____

_____

_____

_____

_____

_____

_____

_____

_____

_____

_____

_____

_____

_____

_____

ACTION STEPS

Write down 3 truths about who you are in Christ:

1. _____
2. _____
3. _____

Identify 3 personal boundaries you need to establish (e.g., not answering toxic calls, limiting time online, protecting quiet time):

1. _____
2. _____
3. _____

Make a list of 5 "Who God Says I Am" affirmations: (Example affirmation: I am chosen.)

1. _____
2. _____
3. _____
4. _____
5. _____

Disengage:

☐ Unfollow or mute toxic sources (social media, TV, relationships)
☐ Remove yourself from conversations that drain you
☐ Replace toxicity with truth-based input Scripture, sermons, positive community)

Start a daily biblical affirmation habit. Use this template:

"Today, I choose to believe I am _____ because God says _____."

REFLECTION SUMMARY

What lies are you replacing with truth in this season?

_____
_____
_____
_____
_____
_____
_____
_____
_____
_____
_____
_____
_____
_____
_____
_____
_____
_____
_____
_____
_____
_____
_____
_____
_____
_____
_____
_____
_____
_____

GROUP ACTIVITY: "TRUTH EXCHANGE"

Option 1: Distribute index cards or use pre-printed "lie/truth" cards.

- Side One: Have each woman write a lie, criticism, or hurtful word they've carried (e.g., "I'm not good enough," "I always fail," "I'll never be loved").

- Side Two: Have each woman flip the card and write a Scripture-based truth to counter the lie (e.g., "I am fearfully and wonderfully made – Psalm 139:14").

- Exchange: Cards are collected anonymously, shuffled, and read aloud by a leader or participant. After each card is read, the group speaks out a communal affirmation like: "We replace that lie with truth!" or "That weapon won't prosper!"

Option 2: Turn this into a spoken word session. Read a chain of lies and immediately follow them with Scripture declarations as a spoken chorus of truth.

Regardless of which option selected, end with a group prayer asking God to rewire their minds, renew their identity, and silence the voice of the enemy.

Use the space below to jot down any key reflections from this group experience.

_____
_____
_____
_____
_____
_____
_____
_____
_____
_____
_____
_____
_____
_____

CHAPTER 6
EMBRACING HOPE & PURPOSE
FROM SURVIVAL TO SIGNIFICANCE

This chapter is an invitation to rise from the ashes of your past with hope as your anchor and purpose as your compass. You are not just surviving—you are becoming. And through faith, healing, and courage, you're being positioned to live with intention, joy, and impact.

* * *

TEACHING MOMENT

Hope is more than optimism—it's spiritual fuel. It's the expectation that God's promises are still in motion, even when you can't yet see the results. Romans 15:13 reminds us that God is the source of hope, and He fills us with joy and peace as we trust Him.

Too often, women stay stuck in survival mode because they're afraid to dream again. But God never designed us to just *get by*. He wants us to thrive. The moment you begin to hope again is the moment you take back your future. When hope rises, so does vision. When purpose is embraced, significance follows. Don't settle for survival—step into the life you were born to lead.

JOURNAL REFLECTION

Reflect on the questions below. Use the lines provided to write honestly and prayerfully.

1. What gives you hope in this season of your life?

_____

_____

_____

_____

_____

_____

_____

_____

2. Reflect on a time when you saw God's faithfulness. How did it encourage you?

_____

_____

_____

_____

_____

_____

_____

_____

3. How do you typically respond when life feels uncertain? What anchors you?

_____

_____

_____

_____

_____

_____

_____

_____

SCRIPTURE MEDITATION

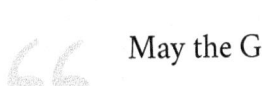

May the God of hope fill you with all joy and peace as you trust in Him…

— ROMANS 15:13

Take a moment to pause, reflect, and handwrite the scripture on the lines below.

_____
_____
_____
_____
_____

What does it look like for your life to be filled with joy and peace, even in the unknown?

_____
_____
_____
_____
_____
_____
_____
_____
_____
_____
_____
_____
_____
_____
_____

ACTION STEPS

List 3 ways God has already provided for you:

1. _____
2. _____
3. _____

Create a gratitude list (write at least 10 things you're thankful for):

1. _____
2. _____
3. _____
4. _____
5. _____
6. _____
7. _____
8. _____
9. _____
10. _____

Choose a new spiritual discipline to begin this month:

□ Morning devotion
□ Scripture memorization
□ Prayer journaling
□ Fasting
□ Serving others
□ Other: _____

Write a daily "Hope Declaration." Use this prompt: (Repeat it aloud each morning.)

"Today I hope for _____ because I believe God will _____."

REFLECTION SUMMARY

How are you embracing both hope and purpose today?

_____

_____

_____

_____

_____

_____

_____

_____

_____

_____

_____

_____

_____

_____

_____

_____

_____

_____

_____

_____

_____

_____

_____

_____

_____

_____

_____

_____

GROUP ACTIVITY: *"HOPE IN ACTION"*

Provide each woman with a sheet of cardstock, scissors, glue sticks, pens, markers, and a table of encouraging magazines, printed scriptures, stickers, or pre-cut affirmations.

Create: Have each participant create a mini Hope Board that reflects the next season of her life. Invite them to include:

- A scripture of hope
- A picture or word representing something they're believing God to do
- A declaration of belief
- Visuals of the life they are building by faith

Share: Once completed, have each woman share one meaningful item or word from her board and explains why it matters to her.

Affirm: As each woman shares, have the group respond with a short affirmation such as: "We believe with you." or "God is faithful to complete it."
Close in prayer covering each vision, asking God to bring it to fruition in His time.

Use the space below to jot down any key reflections from this group experience.

_____
_____
_____
_____
_____
_____
_____
_____
_____
_____
_____
_____
_____

CHAPTER 7
YOUR NEXT STEPS
STEPPING FORWARD IN FAITH

You don't have to have it all figured out to take the next step. Sometimes, the most powerful act of faith is simply moving forward—trusting that God will meet you along the way. This chapter is your invitation to move beyond reflection and into activation. You've walked through healing, you've rediscovered hope, and now it's time to step into purpose with boldness.

Whether your next step is launching a ministry, applying for a new job, joining a support group, or simply saying "yes" to something that scares you—this is your moment. You are not behind. You are right on time. Every chapter of your story has prepared you for this one.

* * *

TEACHING MOMENT

God doesn't call the perfect—He calls the willing. One of the biggest lies the enemy whispers is, *"You're not ready."* But readiness isn't about perfection; it's about surrender. Hebrews 12:1 reminds us to run with perseverance the race marked out for us, letting go of every weight that holds us back.

Your next steps don't have to be big or flashy—they just need to be obedient. When you move in faith, even if it's one small step at a time, God multiplies the impact. This is your race. Your calling. Your moment. Embrace it with open hands and a ready heart. You've been singled out —for such a time as this.

JOURNAL REFLECTION

Reflect on the questions below. Use the lines provided to write honestly and prayerfully.

1. What are your next 3 steps of faith?

_____

_____

_____

_____

_____

_____

_____

_____

2. Who can you support, mentor, or encourage as they walk their journey?

_____

_____

_____

_____

_____

_____

_____

_____

_____

3. What mindset shift must you make in order to move forward?

_____

_____

_____

_____

_____

_____

_____

_____

SCRIPTURE MEDITATION

Let us run with perseverance the race marked out for us...

— HEBREWS 12:1

Take a moment to pause, reflect, and handwrite the scripture on the lines below.

_____

_____

_____

_____

_____

_____

How does this scripture encourage you to stay the course in your unique lane of purpose?

_____

_____

_____

_____

_____

_____

_____

_____

_____

_____

_____

_____

_____

_____

_____

_____

_____

ACTION STEPS

Identify a mentor or an accountability partner:

What's the individual's name? _____

How will they support your journey? _____

_____

_____

Write your 90-day personal or spiritual growth goals:

1. _____
2. _____
3. _____

Choose a scripture to carry into your next season:

Verse: _____

Why it speaks to you: _____

_____

Write a personal letter thanking God's for carrying you thus far:

_____

_____

_____

_____

_____

_____

_____

_____

_____

_____

_____

_____

_____

_____

_____

REFLECTION SUMMARY

What does it mean to live "singled out" on purpose?

_____

_____

_____

_____

_____

_____

_____

_____

_____

_____

_____

_____

_____

_____

_____

_____

_____

_____

_____

_____

_____

_____

_____

_____

_____

_____

_____

_____

_____

_____

GROUP ACTIVITY: *"COMMISSIONING CIRCLE"*

Create a symbolic atmosphere using worship music, Scripture readings, anointing oil, etc. to mark your transition into a new season.

Circle Up: Form a circle with each of the women.
Share: Have each woman shares one next step she's committing to take in faith.

Affirm: After each woman shares, the group affirms her with a spoken blessing such as: "We believe in your purpose," or "You are equipped for this next step."

Bless: The group may choose to pray briefly over each woman or lay hands on shoulders in agreement.

Symbolize:

- Option 1: Light a candle as a symbol of stepping into the light of purpose

- Option 2: Drop a small stone or item in a glass jar to represent letting go and stepping forward

- Option 3: Give each woman a token (key, mustard seed, Scripture card, etc.) to carry with her as a reminder of her purpose

Close with a group declaration: "We step forward in faith. We are not behind. We are chosen, equipped, and commissioned to walk boldly in purpose. Amen."

Use the space below to jot down any key reflections from this group experience.

_____

_____

_____

_____

_____

_____

_____

_____

About the Author

Tiana T. Burnett is a dedicated business owner and real estate investor. She serves on the Board at her local assembly and offers pre-marital support to couples along the East Coast.

Tiana is also the Director of the non-profit BGK Hope Foundation, which empowers children in underprivileged areas by teaching them essential leadership skills.

She currently resides in Maryland, and is happily married with three children.

* * *

To get in touch with Tiana Burnett, please contact her here:
Email: admin@bgkingdom.com